Contents

Introduction

Reading comprehension is the cornerstone of a child's academic success. By completing the activities in this book, children will develop and reinforce essential reading comprehension skills. Children will benefit from a wide variety of opportunities to practice engaging with text as active readers who can self-monitor their understanding of what they have read.

Children will focus on the following:

Identifying the Purpose of the Text
- The reader understands, and can tell you, why they read the text.

Understanding the Text
- What is the main idea of the text?
- What are the supporting details?
- Which parts are facts and which parts are opinions?

Analyzing the Text
- How does the reader's background knowledge enhance the text clues to help the reader answer questions about the text or draw conclusions?
- What inferences can be made by using information from the text with what the reader already knows?
- How does the information from the text help the reader make predictions?
- What is the cause and effect between events?

Making Connections
How does the topic or information they are reading remind the reader about what they already know?
- Text-to-self connections: How does this text relate to your own life?
- Text-to-text connections: Have I read something like this before? How is this text similar to something I have read before? How is this text different from something I have read before?
- Text-to-world connections: What does this text remind you of in the real world?

Using Text Features
- How do different text features help the reader?

Text Features

Text features help the reader to understand the text better. Here is a list of text features with a brief explanation on how they help the reader.

Contents	Here the reader will find the title of each section, what page each text starts on within sections, and where to find specific information.
Chapter Title	The chapter title gives the reader an idea of what the text will be about. The chapter title is often followed by subheadings within the text.
Title and Subheading	The title or topic is found at the top of the page. The subheading is right above a paragraph. There may be more than one subheading in a text.
Map	Maps help the reader understand where something is happening. It is a visual representation of a location.
Diagram and Illustration	Diagrams and illustrations give the reader additional visual information about the text.
Label	A label tells the reader the title of a map, diagram, or illustration. Labels also draw attention to specific elements within a visual.
Caption	Captions are words that are placed underneath the visuals. Captions give the reader more information about the map, diagram, or illustration.
Fact Box	A fact box tells the reader extra information about the topic.
Table	A table presents text information in columns and rows in a concise and often comparative way.
Bold and Italic text	**Bold** and *italic* text are used to emphasize a word or words, and signify that this is important vocabulary.

My Heart

My heart sends blood around my body.

My heart works hard.

I help my heart stay strong and healthy.

The pictures show how.

✔ I exercise.

✔ I eat good food.

I eat fruits and vegetables every day.

✔ I drink lots of water.

I drink about five cups of
water a day.

"My Heart"—Think About It

1. What does the heart do?

_____

2. What does the list in the text help you to know?

_____

3. List three ways to keep the heart strong and healthy.

_____

_____

_____

4. Show how you keep your heart strong. Draw a picture.

5. You can feel your heart work. The picture shows how. Try it. What do you feel?

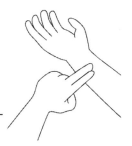

_____

I Can Move My Body

I can move my body in many ways.
I can bend. I can bend low.
I can bend my arm.
I can bend my leg.
I can turn. I can turn right and left.
I can stretch. I can stretch many parts.

Show how your body can move.

Write the words that tell how your body moves.

"I Can Move My Body"—Think About It

1. Who do you think is telling the story? Explain.

_____

_____

2. What do the words *bend*, *turn*, and *stretch* describe?

_____

_____

3. How does the boy move his body in the picture?

_____

4. From the text, you can guess that the boy likes to move. Circle the correct answer.

    A. TRUE

    B. FALSE

We Need Water

We use water in many ways.

Are you thirsty? Water is good to drink when your mouth is dry.

Are you too hot? If you jump in a pool, water will make you feel cooler.

We use water to wash things, too. If you take a bath, water will help you get clean.

Draw a picture of you using water.

Write a sentence about your picture.

"We Need Water"—Think About It

1. What is the main idea of this text?

_____

2. What does the word *thirsty* mean in the text?
   Circle the correct answer.

   A. dry

   B. cold

3. How have you used water today?

_____

_____

4. Which of these can you guess from the text?
   Circle the correct answer.

   A. You can use water to wash a dish.

   B. Water is always cold.

5. Fill in the blanks using words from the text.

   A. Water is good to _____ when your

   mouth is _____.

   B. If you take a _____, water will help

   you get _____.

I Protect Myself from Cold

In the winter, it gets cold.

I wear winter clothes.

First, I put on a warm coat and hat.

Next, I put on mittens.

Then, I place a scarf around my neck.

Finally, I put on boots.

The clothes and boots keep me warm.

If I get too cold, I go inside.

Draw what you wear when it is cold. Show what you like to do in the cold.

Write a sentence about your picture.

"I Protect Myself from Cold" —Think About It

1. What is the main idea?

_____

2. Compare the list and the picture. Are the children dressed for winter?   **YES   NO**   How do you know?

_____

_____

3. What did the author do first to get ready?

_____

4. Which word in the text means "last"? Circle the correct answer.

   A. first

   B. next

   C. finally

5. What should you do if you get too cold?

_____

Cover Sneezes and Coughs

When you have a cold, you sneeze.

When you have a cold, you cough.

Coughing and sneezing spread germs.

Germs make people sick.

You can stop germs from spreading.

When you cough, cover your mouth.

When you sneeze, use a tissue.

If you do not have a tissue, cough or sneeze into your sleeve.

"Cover Sneezes and Coughs"—Think About It

1. How does the title help you understand the text?

_____

_____

2. What happens when you sneeze or cough?

_____

_____

3. What do the pictures help you to learn?

_____

4. List two ways you can stop germs from spreading.

_____

_____

5. What is the author trying to teach the reader?

_____

6. What might you say when a friend sneezes?

_____

No Peanuts for Me!

Some people cannot eat peanuts.

Peanuts make them sick.

Their skin gets red.

Their mouth tingles.

Their throat swells.

They have problems breathing.

They need help. They may need a pill.

They may need a needle.

If you see someone having problems like this, do not wait.

Tell an adult.

"No Peanuts for Me!"—Think About It

1. What does the title of this text mean?

_____

2. List three things that can happen to some people if they eat peanuts.

_____

_____

_____

3. What can you do when someone needs help?

_____

4. What does the picture tell you?

_____

5. How can you keep your classroom free of peanuts?

_____

_____

6. In the text, the word _tingle_ means:

    A. A stinging feeling

    B. To turn blue

Apples Are Good to Eat

Apples are fruit.
They grow on trees.

Apples are a good for you.
They taste good, too.

Some apples are red.
Some apples are green.
Some apples are yellow.

Crunch! It is fun to bite into an apple.
I like to drink apple juice, too.

Draw a picture of how you like to eat apples best.

Write a sentence about your picture.

"Apples Are Good to Eat"—Think About It

1. What is the title of this text?

_____

2. Tell one fact from the text.

_____

3. What does the author say it is fun to do with an apple?

_____

4. All apples are red. Circle the correct answer.

    A. TRUE

    B. FALSE

5. Do you like apples? Why or why not?

_____

_____

6. List different ways to eat apples. Use your own ideas, too.

_____

_____

Safe in the Sun

Sunshine has UV rays. UV rays can burn skin. Protect your skin from UV rays.

✔ Wear sunscreen. Put it on every two hours.

✔ Wear a hat.

✔ Wear sunglasses that stop UV rays.

✔ Stay out of the sunshine. Play in the shade.

Draw how you protect your skin in the sunshine.

Write a sentence about your picture.

"Safe in the Sun"—Think About It

1. What is the text about?

_____

2. Why do we protect skin from UV rays?

_____

3. List four ways to play safely in the sunshine.

_____

_____

_____

4. How often should you put on more sunscreen?

_____

5. Where do you think the girl in the picture is? Explain.

_____

_____

6. What does this text remind you of?

_____

Play Safely

Rules help you play safely. They help you have fun.
Know the rules to play safely outside.

✔ Wait your turn.

✔ Sit down on swings and slides.

✔ Tie up your shoes.

✔ Wear sunscreen.

✔ Be careful when it is wet.

Play safely on a slide.

Hold on to climb up.

Make sure the slide is clear before you go.

Sit down to slide.

"Play Safely"—Think About It

1. Why do we need rules?

_____

2. What are two rules for playing safely outside?

_____

_____

3. Pam does not follow the rules on the slide. What can happen? Circle the correct answer.

   A. Pam can get hurt.

   B. Pam can get wet.

4. Draw a picture. Show how to play safely on a swing.

What Is a Smoke Detector?

A smoke detector tells you when there is smoke from something burning.

When there is smoke, a smoke detector starts to beep very loudly. This warns people that there may be a fire.

What should you do when a smoke detector is beeping loudly?

Here is what to do:

First, go outside.
Next, find an adult.
Finally, ask for help.

Draw what to do when a smoke detector beeps.

Write a sentence about your picture.

"What Is a Smoke Detector?"
—Think About It

1. What does a smoke detector do?

_____

2. What sound does it make?

_____

3. How does the checklist help you understand the text?

_____

4. If you hear a smoke detector, what do you do:

First, _____

Next, _____

Finally, _____

5. Circle TRUE or FALSE for each statement.

A smoke detector lets you
know when dinner is ready.   A. TRUE   B. FALSE

A smoke detector
beeps loudly.   A. TRUE   B. FALSE

Who Keeps Me Safe?

Many people keep me safe.

Police protect me. They help when I am lost. They stop bad people, too.

Firefighters help when there is a fire. Fires could hurt me. Firefighters put out fires.

Doctors help when I am sick. They take care of me.

Nurses help when I am sick, too.

Police Officer

Firefighter

Doctor

Nurse

"Who Keeps Me Safe?"—Think About It

1. How do police protect you?

_____

2. How do firefighters protect you?

_____

3. How do doctors and nurses help you?

_____

4. How do the pictures help tell the text?

_____

5. Draw a time when someone kept you safe.

```
┌─────────────────────────────────────────┐
│                                           │
│                                           │
│                                           │
│                                           │
│                                           │
│                                           │
│                                           │
│                                           │
│                                           │
└─────────────────────────────────────────┘
```

Write a sentence about your picture.

_____

Inky Dinky Spider

Have fun with this song. Sing it fast. Sing it slow.

Inky dinky spider

Climbed up the water spout.

Down came the rain,

And washed the spider out.

Out came the sun,

And dried up all the rain.

And the inky dinky spider

Climbed up the spout again.

Draw a picture of what happened when the sun came out.

"Inky Dinky Spider"—Think About It

1. What is the song about?

_____

2. Tell what happens in the song.

First, _____

Next, _____

Then, _____

Finally, _____

3. What dried up all the rain?

_____

4. Do you like this song? Explain why or why not.

_____

_____

5. Inky dinky spider is washed down the water spout by snow. Circle the correct answer.

   A. TRUE

   B. FALSE

One, Two, Buckle My Shoe

Have fun with this chant. Say it fast. Say it slow. Act it out.

One, two,
Buckle my shoe.

Three, four,
Shut the door.

Five, six,
Pick up sticks.

Seven, eight,
Lay them straight.

Nine, ten,
A big, fat hen.

"One, Two, Buckle My Shoe"
—Think About It

1. What is the title of the chant?

_____

2. Look at the picture. What does "buckle my shoe" mean?

_____

3. What is the highest number in the chant?

_____

4. What action do you do with three, four?

_____

5. _Two_ and _shoe_ rhyme. They end with the same sound.
Find two other words that rhyme.

_____

6. Fill in the blanks.

One, two, _____ my shoe,

Three, four, _____ the door,

Five, six, pick up _____,

Seven, eight, lay them _____,

Nine, ten, a big, _____ _____.

Where Does Trash Go?

People make a lot of trash.
A truck picks the trash up.

Most trash goes to a
landfill. Machines dig dirt
to cover the trash.

This truck is picking up trash
to take to the landfill.

The landfill can get full. When the landfull is full, where
will the trash go? You can help by making less trash.

This machine is moving around trash in a landfill.

"Where Does Trash Go?"—Think About It

1. What is a *landfill*? How do you know?

_____

2. Write one fact you know about landfills.

_____

3. What does each picture show?

_____

4. What can you do to make less trash? Put a ✔.

☐ Use both sides of paper.

☐ Give clothes that do not fit you to smaller kids.

☐ Save leftover food for snacks.

5. Draw a picture of what you do to make less trash.

Farmers

Farmers grow food. They sow seeds and care for plants. They pick fruits and vegetables.

Farmer picking apples

Farmers take care of animals. Chickens give eggs and meat. Cows give milk and meat.

Farmer taking care of her cows

Truck drivers take the food to stores.

Truck driver carrying vegetables

Store clerks sell the food.

Clerk selling food

"Farmers"—Think About It

1. What do farmers grow?

_____

2. Where does meat come from?

_____

3. Who takes the food to the stores?

_____

4. Who sells you food?

_____

5. Draw a picture of your family cooking food together.
   Show what you are cooking.

_____

Write a sentence about your picture.

_____

At the Park

There is a park near my home.
I love going to the park.

At the park, I play on the slide first.
Then I swing on the swings.

There is a tall tree at the park.
I like to sit under the tree.

I have fun at the park

Draw what you like to do at the park.

Write a sentence about your picture.

"At the Park"—Think About It

1. What does the title tell you about the text?

_____

2. Where is the park?

_____

3. What happens first in the text?

_____

4. Do you like to go to a park? Why or why not?

_____

_____

5. Why do you think the author likes going to the park?

_____

_____

6. Fill in the blanks using words from the text.

A. At the park, I play on the _____ first.

B. Then I _____ on the swings.

Out on the Lake

I like to go out on the lake in a boat.
The water is blue.
I see fish in the water.

Some days there are lots of boats.
Some days there is just our boat.

I love to be out on the lake.
Being out on the lake on a summer day is fun!

Draw a picture of yourself out on a lake.

Write a sentence about your picture.

"Out on the Lake"—Think About It

1. What is the title of this text?

_____

2. What does the author see in the water?

_____

3. What is an opinion from the story?

_____

_____

4. List three things you can do at a lake.

_____

_____

_____

5. What does the author say in the text about boats on the lake?

_____

The Sun

Every morning the Sun rises.
The Sun rises in the sky.

The Sun gives us light.
The Sun also gives us heat.

When you first get up, it may be cool outside.
As the Sun rises, the day gets warmer.
As the Sun rises, the day also gets brighter.

I love the warm sunshine on my skin!

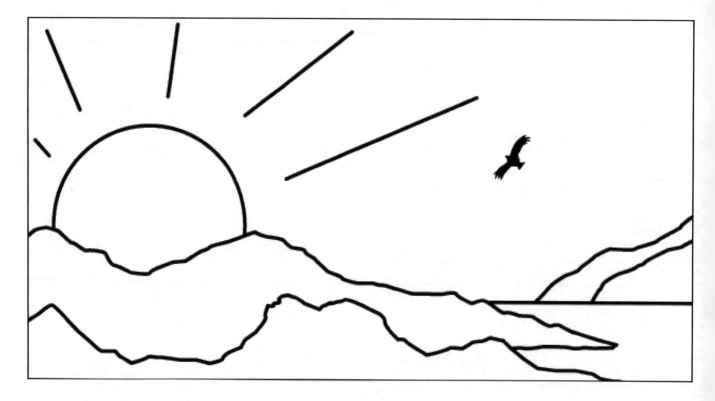

"The Sun"—Think About It

1. What is the text about?

_____

2. Which sentence is a fact from the text?
Circle the correct answer.

A. Every morning the Sun rises.

B. The Moon shines at night.

3. Which is an opinion from the text?
Circle the correct answer.

A. The Sun gives us light.

B. I love the warm sunshine on my skin!

4. The Sun gives us heat. Circle the correct answer.

A. TRUE

B. FALSE

5. What happens first in the text?
Circle the correct answer.

A. The Sun rises.

B. The day gets warmer.

Space

At night, the sky is dark.
At night, I can see space.

I can see the Moon in space.
I can see stars in space.
Sometimes, I can see shooting stars.

Did you know that there are planets in space?

Draw what you can see in space.

Write a sentence about your picture.

"Space"—Think About It

1. What is the title of this text?

_____

2. Circle the fact from the text.

    A. I can see balloons in the sky.

    B. I can see stars in space.

3. Planets are in space. Circle the correct answer.

    A. TRUE

    B. FALSE

4. What do the words _shooting star_ mean?
Circle the correct answer.

    A. A star that moves quickly across the sky.

    B. A star that you see every night in the sky.

5. List three things the author can see in space.

_____

_____

_____

About Seeds

A seed is a tiny plant waiting to grow.

A peanut is a seed.

A coconut is a seed.

Dandelion seeds have fluff on them.

Maple tree seeds have wings.

Sun, water, and soil help seeds
grow into plants.

Dandelions

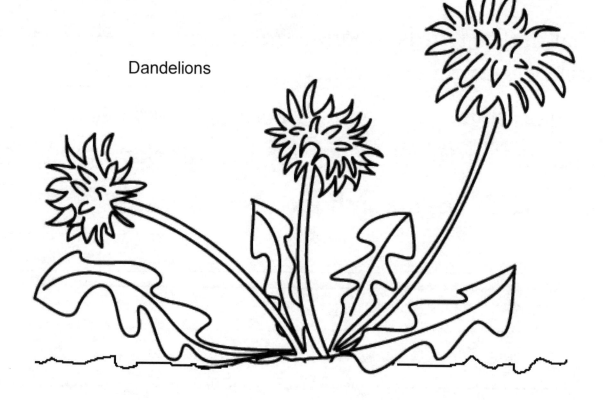

"About Seeds"—Think About It

1. What does the text tell you a seed is?

_____

2. Name three things that help seeds to grow into plants.

_____

_____

_____

3. Some seeds have special parts that help them fly. Name the two special parts talked about in the text.

_____

_____

4. List two types of seeds from the text.

_____

_____

5. Which fact did you learn from the text?
   Circle the correct answer.

   A. Seeds need sun, water, and soil to grow.

   B. All seeds grow into plants that have flowers.

What Is a Cactus?

A cactus is a type of plant.

Most cactuses do not have leaves.

Instead, they have sharp needles called spines.

Most cactuses live in the desert.

It does not rain much in the desert.

Cactuses do not need much water.

"What Is a Cactus?"—Think About It

1. What new things did you learn from this text?

_____

2. Is a cactus a plant or an animal?

_____

3. Where do most cactuses live?

_____

4. What are *spines*?

_____

5. What does the word *desert* mean?
   Circle the correct answer.

   A. A place where it snows a lot.

   B. A place where it does not rain much.

6. Draw a picture of a cactus in the desert or in a planter.

Sara's Flower Garden

Sara has a flower garden.
She plants seeds in the soil with care.

Sara waters the seeds.
The water helps the seeds grow into tall plants.
The sunshine helps the plants grow, too.

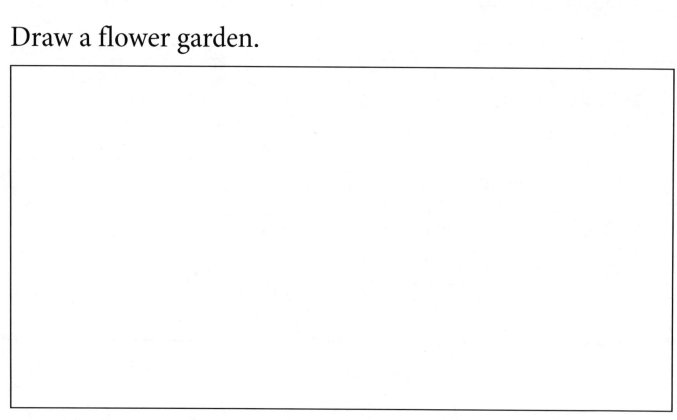

Sara's plants grow flowers.
Sara is happy.
She likes the red flowers best!

Draw a flower garden.

What kinds of flowers would you plant?

"Sara's Flower Garden"—Think About It

1. What two things does Sara do with the seeds?

_____

_____

2. Which sentence is a fact from the text? Circle the correct answer.

    A. Sara has a flower garden.

    B. Sara has an orange cat.

3. Do you think Sara likes her garden? How do you know?

_____

_____

4. What happens after Sara waters the seeds?

_____

_____

5. Sara likes the blue flowers best. Circle the correct answer.

    A. TRUE

    B. FALSE

How People Use Plants

People use plants in many ways.

Apples, carrots, chocolate, and many other foods come from plants.

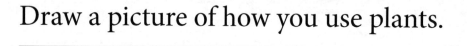

Trees are plants.
Wood comes from trees.
People burn wood for heat.
Some houses are made from wood.
Hockey sticks and baseball bats are made from wood, too!

Draw a picture of how you use plants.

Write a sentence about your picture.

"How People Use Plants"—Think About It

1. What is the main idea of this text?

_____

2. Trees are plants. Circle the correct answer.

    A. TRUE

    B. FALSE

3. What are your favourite things to eat that come from plants?

_____

_____

4. List two facts about plants from the text.

_____

_____

5. What is a detail from the text to show how people use wood?

_____

_____

Why Plant a Tree?

Trees help us in many ways.

Trees clean the air we breathe.

Trees protect us from the sun and wind.

Trees give animals a place to live and food to eat.

Some trees give us food.

Many fruits and nuts grow on trees.

"Why Plant a Tree?"—Think About It

1. How do trees change the air?

_____

2. What do trees protect you from?

_____

3. How do trees help animals?

_____

4. What tree foods do you eat?

_____

5. What does the picture show?

_____

6. List four ways trees help.

_____

_____

_____

How to Be a Good Friend

I treat my friends the way I like to be treated.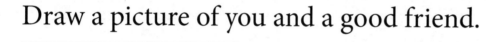

✔ I am kind to them.

✔ I listen to what they say.

✔ I stick up for them.

✔ I share my toys and games with them.

✔ I take turns when I play games with them.

✔ I play fair with them.

Draw a picture of you and a good friend.

Write a sentence about why they are a good friend to you.

"How to Be a Good Friend"—Think About It

1. What is the author trying to teach the reader?

_____

2. List four ways to be a good friend.

_____

_____

_____

_____

3. Which item on the list does the picture show?

_____

4. Your friend has a hat you like. What could you say to your friend?

_____

5. What is an example of how to be kind to a friend?

_____

_____

Ways to Be Kind

Be kind to others.

✔ Smile and say hello.

✔ Say please and thank you.

✔ Listen to what they say.

✔ Help them when they need help.

✔ Tell them when they do well.

How does the picture show kindness?

"Ways to Be Kind"—Think About It

1. What other title could you give the text?

_____

2. What does the picture show?

_____

_____

3. Trace your hand. On each finger, write a way to show kindness.

4. Put a ✔ for each way that shows kindness.

☐ Argue.

☐ Take care of a friend's toys.

☐ Carry a package for my mother.

☐ Call someone names.

Play Fair

Val plays tag with friends.
Jon is "It." He tags Val.
Val starts to get mad.
Then she stops.
Val counts to 10.

Val plays fair. She is "It."
She runs after her friends.
Val is a good sport.
It is fun to play with Val.

"Play Fair"—Think About It

1. What is the main idea of the text?

_____

2. It is not fun to play tag with Val.

    A. TRUE

    B. FALSE

How do you know?

_____

_____

3. When is someone a good sport? Which cartoon shows a good sport?

_____

4. How did Val play fair?

_____

5. Draw a picture of a game you play. Show how you play fair.

Julie Payette

As a little girl, Julie Payette watched space missions on TV.

She wanted to be an astronaut, too.

When Julie grew up, she trained to go into space.

She learned to fly two types of planes.

Julie also flew in a very special plane.

Being in the plane was like being in space.

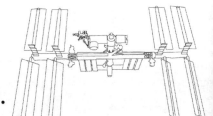

International Space Station

Julie went to space two times.

She went on the International Space Station.

Julie was the first Canadian to go on the Space Station.

She liked being an astronaut.

Draw what you want to be when you grow up.

Write a sentence about your picture.

"Julie Payette"—Think About It

1. What made Julie want to be an astronaut? Circle the correct answer.

   A. Watching cartoons on TV.
   B. Watching space missions on TV.

2. Julie flew in a very special plane. Use the text to explain why the plane was special.

   _____

   _____

3. In the text, what does the word *astronaut* mean? Circle the correct answer.

   A. Someone who travels in space.
   B. Someone who likes ice cream.

4. Julie was the first Canadian to do something exciting. What did she do? Circle the correct answer.

   A. Go on the International Space Station.
   B. Travel to the Moon.

5. What did Julie learn to do as part of her training to go into space?

   _____

Chris Hadfield

When Chris Hadfield was a boy,
he wanted to travel in space.
When Chris grew up, he did
travel in space!
Chris became an astronaut.

Chris Hadfield played his guitar in space.

Chris showed people what it is like to live in space.
He brushed his teeth in space.
He sang in space.

Chris took many pictures in space.
He showed people what Earth looks like from space.

Draw a picture of what you think Chris saw from space.

Write a sentence about your picture.

"Chris Hadfield"—Think About It

1. What is Chris Hadfield's job?

_____

2. What does the caption on the picture say Chris did in space?

_____

3. Would you like to go to space? Why or why not?

_____

_____

4. Chris travelled in space when he was a boy. Circle the correct answer.

A. TRUE

B. FALSE

5. Which sentence is a fact from the text? Circle the correct answer.

A. Chris drew many pictures in space.

B. Chris took many pictures in space.

Alexander Graham Bell

Alexander Graham Bell liked to invent things and build machines.

When he was a boy, Alexander built things. He wanted to know how machines worked.

When he grew up, Alexander liked helping people.

A telephone from 1919

Alexander invented the very first telephone. The telephone helps people talk to each other.

Draw the type of phone you use.

Is your phone the same as the picture? How is it different?

"Alexander Graham Bell"—Think About It

1. Who is this text about?

_____

2. What does the word _invent_ mean?

_____

_____

3. Circle the sentence that is a fact from the text.

   A. Alexander invented the telephone.

   B. Alexander invented the car.

4. What types of things did Alexander like to do?

_____

_____

5. Alexander was a nice man. How can you tell?

_____

_____

My Trip to a Farm

FROM: Kyle

TO: Grandma

I went to a farm. I saw cows and pigs. I collected eggs.
I walked in the corn maze.
I picked some apples. I put them in a basket.
Maybe we can make a pie.

Love,
Kyle

"My Trip to the Farm"—Think About It

1. Who wrote the email? How do you know?

_____

_____

2. Who will get the email?

_____

3. Who is telling the story? How do you know?

_____

_____

4. Where did Kyle go?

_____

5. Draw what Kyle asked his grandmother to make.

What Animals Eat

All animals need food to grow and to stay alive.

Some animals eat plants.

Moose eat water plants and soft branches.

Rabbits snack on plant buds and leaves.

Many birds munch seeds from plants.

Some animals eat meat.

Bears and lions eat meat.

Some birds such as eagles and hawks eat meat, too.

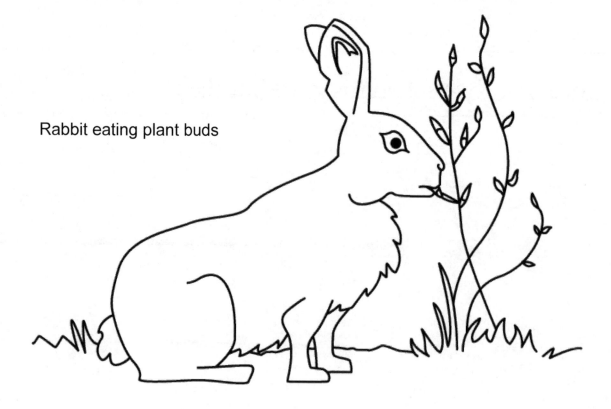

Rabbit eating plant buds

"What Animals Eat"—Think About It

1. Why do animals need to eat food?

_____

2. List two different foods that animals eat.

_____

_____

3. What does the word *munch* mean?
Circle the correct answer.

   A. To drink

   B. To eat

4. Bears eat twigs. Circle the correct answer.

   A. TRUE

   B. FALSE

5. Draw a picture of an animal eating food.

Taking Care of a Pet

Do you want a pet?

Here is how to take care of one.

✔ Feed the pet every day.

✔ Make sure the pet has water.

✔ Give the pet exercise.

✔ Play with the pet.

✔ Be kind to the pet.

✔ Take it to a veterinarian when the pet is sick.

Draw a picture showing how to take care of a pet.

Write a sentence about your picture.

"Taking Care of a Pet"—Think About It

1. What is the main idea of the text?

_____

_____

2. Give three details from the text.

_____

_____

_____

3. What does a veterinarian do?

_____

_____

_____

4. If you were a veterinarian, what kinds of animals would you like to help? Explain your thinking.

_____

_____

_____

My Cat Boots

Boots is my cat.
She is brown with white feet.
Boots likes to play.
She chases little balls.

My cat Boots likes me to feed her.
She tells me when she wants to eat.

First, Boots meows.
Next, she jumps up on my lap.
Then, I go and get some cat food.
Finally, I feed Boots.

"My Cat Boots"—Think About It

1. What is the text about?

_____

2. List two things that Boots likes to do.

_____

_____

3. What two things does Boots do when she wants to be fed?

_____

_____

4. Draw a picture of Boots doing something she likes to do.

My Dog Jake

Jake is my little black dog.
He is the best pet ever!

Jake can do many tricks.
He can shake hands.
He can play catch.

I like to take Jake for walks.
Walking helps keep Jake healthy.
I love to play with Jake!

Draw a picture of your dog or a pet you would like to have.

Write a sentence about your picture.

"My Dog Jake"—Think About It

1. What special things can Jake do?

_____

_____

2. Which sentence can you find in the text?
Circle the correct answer.

A. Jake is the best pet ever.

B. Jake can do many tricks.

3. What does the author say about Jake?
Circle the correct answer.

A. I love to play with Jake.

B. He is the best pet ever!

4. Would you like a pet dog? Tell why or why not.

_____

_____

_____

Ducks and Geese

Ducks and geese both have wings and feathers.
Ducks are smaller than geese.

Geese are mostly white, grey, black, or brown.
Ducks can be many different colours.

Ducks like to swim in the water.
Geese also like to swim in the water.

Draw a picture of a duck or goose.

Write a sentence about your picture.

_____

"Ducks and Geese"—Think About It

1. What kind of animals are ducks and geese? What are the clues in the text?

_____

_____

_____

2. What is a detail in the text about ducks?

_____

3. What is a detail in the text about geese?

_____

4. Tell one way that ducks and geese are alike.

_____

5. Tell one way that ducks and geese are different.

_____

6. Fill in the blanks using words from the text.

A. Ducks and geese both have _____

and _____.

Fish Facts

Fish live in the water.
Fish live in lakes, ponds, rivers, and oceans.

Fish swim in the water.
Fish flap their fins and tail to swim.
Their fins and tail make them move.

Some fish are flat.
Other fish are round.
Some fish are long and thin.

Sharks are fish.
Tuna are fish, too.

A shark

"Fish Facts"—Think About It

1. Where do fish live?

_____

2. How do fish move?

_____

3. Would you like a pet fish? Why or why not?

_____

4. Tuna are fish. Circle the correct answer.

   A. TRUE

   B. FALSE

5. Draw a fish.

Describe the fish.

Mighty Moles

Moles are small, furry animals.
They have short legs with sharp claws.

Moles are good diggers.
They live in tunnels in the ground.

Moles have tiny eyes and ears.
They cannot see or hear well.

Moles eat worms, bugs, and mice.

Draw a picture of a mole in its home using details from the text.

Write a sentence to describe your picture.

"Mighty Moles"—Think About It

1. What does the title tell you about moles?

_____

2. A mole has a thick, furry coat. Would the mole's furry coat help the mole stay warm or stay cool?

_____

3. Moles are large animals. Circle the correct answer.

A. TRUE

B. FALSE

4. From the text, which of these can you guess?
Circle the correct answer.

A. Worms live in the ground.

B. Moles eat birds.

5. Which sentence is a fact from the text?
Circle the correct answer.

A. Moles have sharp claws.

B. Moles have tiny mouths.

6. What three things do moles eat?

_____   _____   _____

You Can Write an Email

An email has four parts.

The first line shows your email address.
The second line shows your friend's address.

The subject line tells what the email is about.

The message is what you write in the email.
Your name goes at the end of the email.

"You Can Write an Email"—Think About It

1. What is this text about?

_____

2. Label the picture. Use these words.

addresses   message   your name   subject

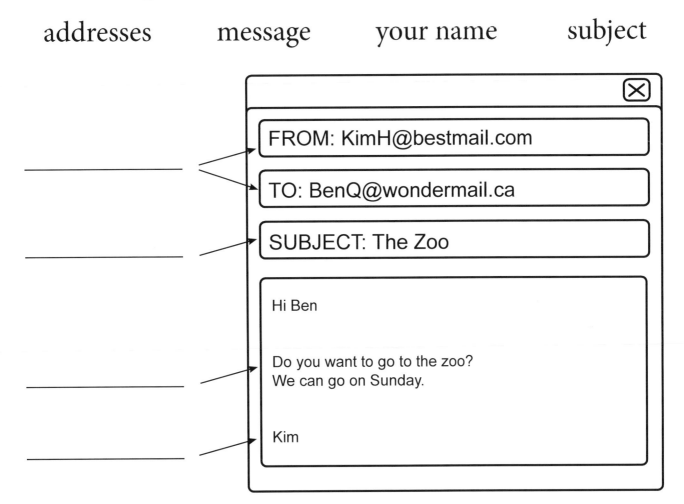

FROM: KimH@bestmail.com

TO: BenQ@wondermail.ca

SUBJECT: The Zoo

Hi Ben

Do you want to go to the zoo?
We can go on Sunday.

Kim

3. Who do you know that writes emails? Tell about it.

_____

_____

You Can Write a Postcard

The postcard is from Ottawa.

Ottawa is the capital of Canada.

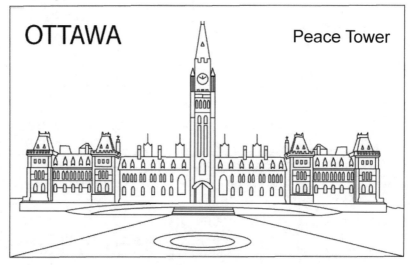

Look at the back of the postcard.

The postcard has a message.

The postcard has a place to sign your name.

The address tells where to send the postcard.

The stamp pays the post office to send the postcard.

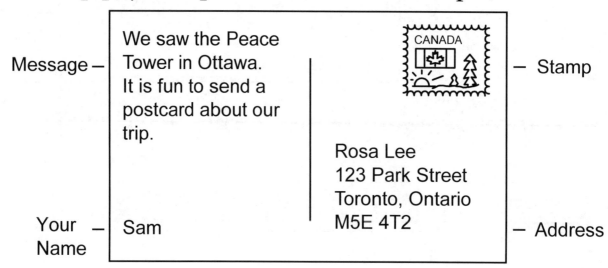

"You Can Write a Postcard"
—Think About It

1. What does the postcard show?

_____

2. What place have you visited? Draw a picture.

3. Write a postcard about the place you visited.

4. Cut out your postcard. Glue the sides together.

5. Give the postcard to a family member.

This Is January

January is a month. It is the first month in the year.

January 1 starts the year. January has 31 days.

A calendar shows the days in January.

Each day has a number.

Pam has a birthday in January.

SUNDAY	MONDAY	TUESDAY	WEDNESDAY	THURSDAY	FRIDAY	SATURDAY
			1 New Year's Day	2	3	4
5	6	7	8	9	10	11
12	13	14	15	16	17 PAM	18
19	20	21	22	23	24	25
26	27	28	29	30	31	

January

"This Is January"—Think About It

1. Does the picture show what the words say?   **YES   NO**
Explain.

_____

2. What month starts the year? How many days does it have?

_____

3. When is Pam's birthday?

_____

4. New Year's Day is in January. What other holiday is in January?

_____

5. Label your birthday month on the calendar. Add the numbers. Circle your birthday.

MONTH:						
SUNDAY	MONDAY	TUESDAY	WEDNESDAY	THURSDAY	FRIDAY	SATURDAY

Summer Days

I love summer!
Summer days are sunny and hot.
The summer sky is blue.

Sometimes my family goes to the beach in summer.
I play on the sand near the water.
I like looking for shells in the sand.

I go swimming in the water.
Sometimes I see fish in the water.

"Summer Days"—Think About It

1. Which sentence is a fact from the text?

    A. Summer days are sunny and hot.

    B. Winter days are cold.

2. Do you think the author likes summer? How do you know?

_____

3. What does the author like to look for on the beach?

_____

4. What does the author see in the water?

_____

5. Draw a picture of your family at the beach.

One Fall Day

I love the fall.
It is the best season.
The sky is blue.
The air is cool.

I put on a sweater.
I go outside.

I play in the leaves. They are red and yellow.
Then I help my mom rake the leaves.
After, we drink hot chocolate.

Draw a picture of your favourite thing to do in the fall. Use fall colours.

Write a sentence about your picture.

"One Fall Day"—Think About It

1. What is the text about?

_____

2. What type of clothing does the person in the text wear outside on a fall day?

_____

3. What colours are the fall leaves?

_____

4. What other colours of leaves have you seen in the fall?

_____

5. How does the author help their mom?

_____

6. Do you agree with the author fall is the best season? Explain.

_____

_____

_____

How Toy Ads Work

Look at a toy ad.

It makes you want to buy the toy.

The ad has words and pictures.

The pictures make you look at the ad.

The words make the toy seem to be lots of fun.

Do you need a new toy to have fun?

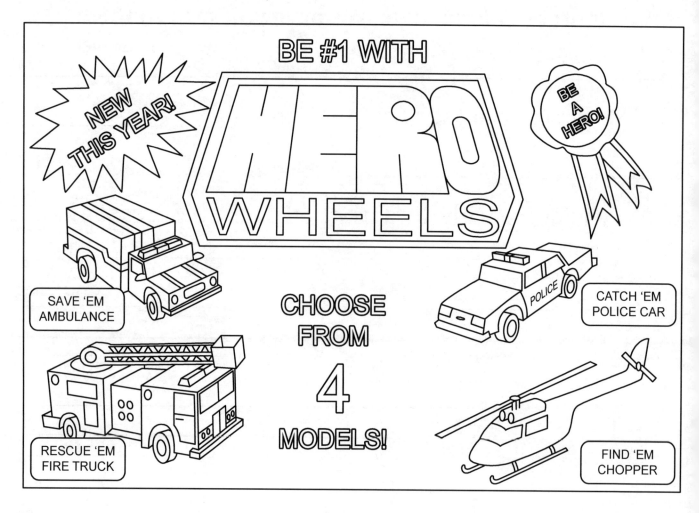

"How Toy Ads Work"—Think About It

1. What is the ad selling?

_____

2. How does the ad get your attention?

_____

3. What does the ad say?

_____

4. Does the author tell a story or give information?
How do you know?

_____

_____

5. Does the picture show what the words say? **YES   NO**
Explain.

_____

_____

6. Fill in the blanks using words from the text.

A. The ad has _____ and _____.

B. The pictures make you _____ at the _____.

I Have Money

5¢

I have five coins.

One is worth 5 cents.

One is worth 10 cents.

10¢

One is worth 25 cents.

One is worth 1 dollar.

One is worth 2 dollars.

25¢

100¢ or $1

200¢ or $2

"I Have Money"—Think About It

1. What is the main idea of the text?

_____

2. How do the pictures help you understand the text?

_____

3. What is different about the text and the pictures?

_____

4. How many coins are there?

_____

5. What is each coin worth?
What is the total?

_____

6. You have 30¢. Show the coins you have.

Mixing Colours

You can mix colours to make new colours.

Get some paint and and try it!

Mix red and yellow. You get orange.

Red and white make pink.

Yellow and blue make green.

Blue and red make purple.

What other colours can you make?

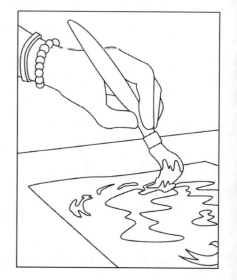

Draw a rainbow.

What is your favourite colour? Why do you like that colour?

"Mixing Colours"—Think About It

1. What is the author trying to teach the reader?

_____

2. What four colours do you need to mix the paints?

_____   _____

_____   _____

3. What happens when you mix yellow and blue?

_____

4. Draw and colour a picture that shows how to make purple.

5. Red + yellow = orange. Write the sentence for making pink.

_____

Clouds

I like to watch clouds.
They float in the sky.

Some clouds are white.
White clouds can be round and fluffy.

Some clouds are grey.
Grey clouds can bring rain and snow.

Look at clouds when the sun is setting in the evening.
Evening clouds can turn pink and blue.

"Clouds"—Think About It

1. What is the main idea of this text?

_____

2. Do you like to watch clouds? Why or why not?

_____

_____

3. Do all clouds bring rain? How do you know?

_____

_____

4. Circle TRUE or FALSE.

Some clouds are green.	A. TRUE	B. FALSE
Some clouds bring rain or snow.	A. TRUE	B. FALSE
Clouds float in the sky.	A. TRUE	B. FALSE

5. When can you see clouds that are pink and blue?

_____

_____

Make Some Noise!

Do you like to sing the song "Happy Birthday"?
It is fun to sing and make noise.

On New Year's Eve, people yell "Happy New Year!"
People blow party horns, too.

Fireworks are fun to watch.
Fireworks make a lot of noise!

Draw a picture of fireworks.

Do you like fireworks? Why or why not?

"Make Some Noise!"—Think About It

1. Which sentence is a fact from the text?
  Circle the correct answer.

  A. On New Year's Eve, people yell "Happy Birthday!"

  B. On New Year's Eve, people yell "Happy New Year!"

2. Do you think fireworks are fun to watch?
  Why or why not?

_____

_____

3. What do you like to do on your birthday?

_____

4. List four things people do on New Year's Eve.

_____

_____

_____

_____

Using Text Features— Table of Contents

Table of Contents

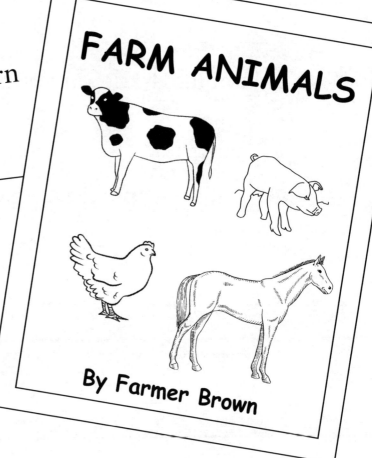

FARM ANIMALS

By Farmer Brown

"Using Text Features—Table of Contents" —Think About It

1. What is the title of the book?

_____

2. Who is the author of the book?

_____

3. How many chapters are in the book?

_____

4. What is the title of Chapter 5?

_____

5. What is the title of Chapter 2?

_____

6. Which chapter tells about the barn?

_____

7. Which chapter is about cows?

_____

8. What is Chapter 3 about?

_____

Graphic Organizers

Graphic organizers are excellent tools to use for identify and organizing information from a text into an easy-to-understand visual format. Students will expand their comprehension of a text as they complete the graphic organizers. Use these graphic organizers in addition to the activities in this book or with other texts.

Concept Web – Helps students understand the main idea of a text and how it is supported by key details.

Concept Map – Helps students gain a better understanding of how different subtopics within a text connect to the topic as a whole.

Venn Diagram/Comparison Chart – Helps students focus on the comparison of two items, such as individuals, ideas, events, or pieces of information. Students could compare by looking at which things are the same, or contrast by looking at which things are different.

Fact or Opinion – Helps students to distinguish between statements of fact or opinion. Facts are pieces of information that can be proven to be true. Opinions are pieces of information based on something that someone thinks or believes, but that cannot necessarily be proven to be true.

Cause and Effect – Helps students to recognize and explain relationships between events. The cause is the reason why an event happens and the effect is the event that happens.

Making Connections – Helps students to connect something they have read, or experienced, with the world around them.

Context Clue Chart – Helps students organize clues that the author gives in a text to help define a difficult or unusual word. Encourage students to look for explanations of words within a text.

Drawing Conclusions and Making Inferences Chart – Helps students practice drawing conclusions and making inferences based on their prior knowledge, as well as what they read in the text.

A Concept Web About...

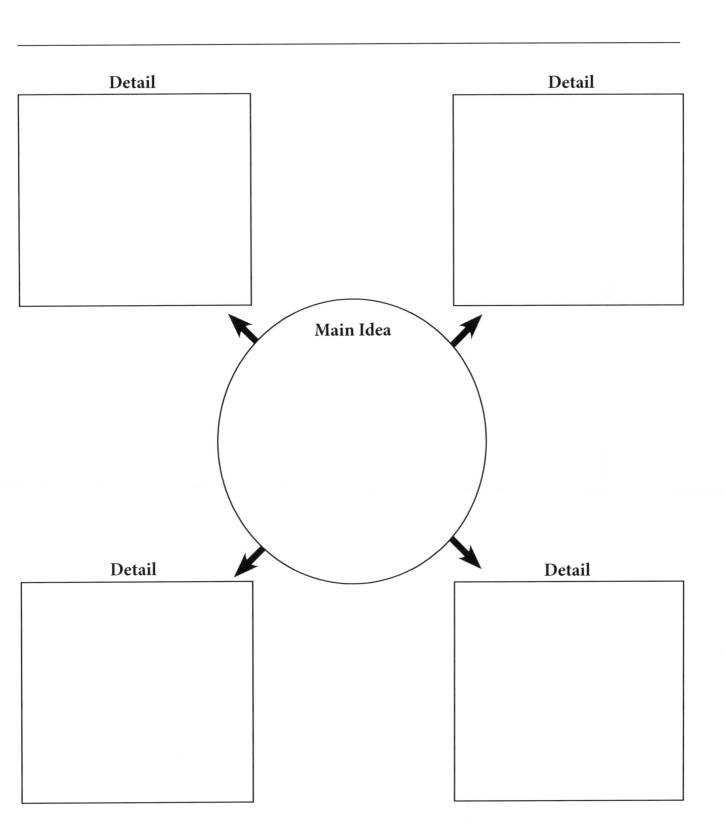

Detail

Detail

Main Idea

Detail

Detail

Concept Map

A **main idea** is what the text is mostly about.
A **subheading** is the title given to a part of a text.
A **detail** is important information that tells more about the main idea.

Main Idea

Subheading

Subheading

Details

Details

A Venn Diagram About...

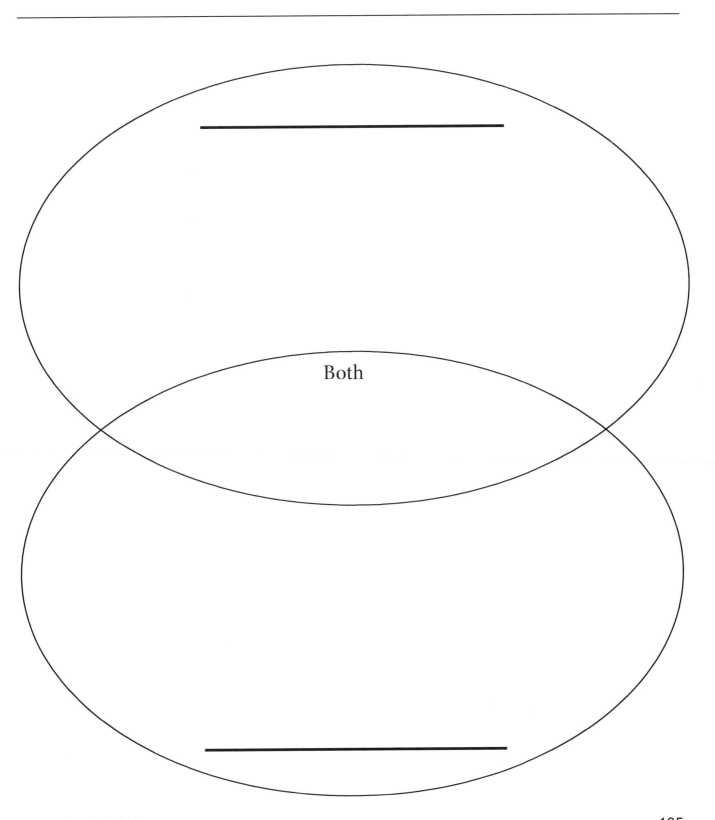

Both

A Comparison Chart

Compared
to

Detailed information

Detailed information

Fact or Opinion

- Facts are pieces of information that can be proven to be true.
- Opinions are pieces of information based on something a person thinks or believes.

Piece of Information	Fact or Opinion?	How do you know?

Cause and Effect

- The **cause** is the reason something happens.
- The **effect** is what happened.

Effect

Cause

Making Connections with What I Have Read

After reading...	It reminds me of...	This helps me make a connection to...
		☐ something else I have read ☐ myself ☐ the world around me
		☐ something else I have read ☐ myself ☐ the world around me

Context Clue Chart

Context Clues are hints that the author gives in a text that can help you find the meaning of a word.

Word	Context Clue from Text	Meaning of Word

110

Drawing Conclusions and Making Inferences Chart

We make an **inference** when we combine what we know to be true with new information and come to a conclusion.

What I already know:

Clues from the text I read:

What I can conclude or infer:

How Am I Doing?

	Completing my work	Using my time wisely	Following directions	Keeping organized
Full speed ahead!	• My work is always complete and done with care. • I added extra details to my work.	• I always get my work done on time.	• I always follow directions.	• My materials are always neatly organized. • I am always prepared and ready to learn.
Keep going!	• My work is complete and done with care. • I added extra details to my work.	• I usually get my work done on time.	• I usually follow directions without reminders.	• I usually can find my materials. • I am usually prepared and ready to learn.
Slow down!	• My work is complete. • I need to check my work.	• I sometimes get my work done on time.	• I sometimes need reminders to follow directions.	• I sometimes need time to find my materials. • I am sometimes prepared and ready to learn.
Stop!	• My work is not complete. • I need to check my work.	• I rarely get my work done on time.	• I need reminders to follow directions.	• I need to organize my materials. • I am rarely prepared and ready to learn.

Reading Comprehension Student Tracking Sheet

Student's Name	Identifies the Purpose of the Text *Student: I can tell you why we read this.*	Demonstrates Understanding of the Text *Student: I can tell you what the text is about.*	Analyzes Text *Student: I can make predictions, interpretations, and conclusions using information from the text.*	Makes Connections to Text (Prior Knowledge) *Student: This reminds me of* • text to text • text to self • text to world	Text Features *Student: I can tell you how different text features help the reader.*

Level 4: Student shows a thorough understanding of all or almost all concepts and consistently gives appropriate and complete explanations independently. No teacher support is needed.

Level 3: Student shows a good understanding of most concepts and usually gives complete or nearly complete explanations. Infrequent teacher support is needed.

Level 2: Student shows a satisfactory understanding of most concepts and sometimes gives appropriate but incomplete explanations. Teacher support is sometimes needed.

Level 1: Student shows little of understanding of concepts and rarely gives complete explanations. Intensive teacher support is needed.

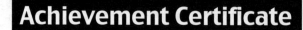

Achievement Certificate

You Are Doing Well!

Keep Up the Good Work!

_____
Name

_____
Date

Reading Comprehension

Answers

My Heart, pp. 4–5
1. The heart sends blood around the body.
2. The list helps me know what the girl does to keep her heart healthy and strong.
3. Three ways to keep the heart strong and healthy are exercise, eat good foods (fruits and vegetables), and drink lots of water.
4. Ensure that students show themselves exercising and/or eating proper foods.
5. Answers may vary. Students should say they feel a steady beat or pulse.

I Can Move My Body, pp. 6–7
1. Sample answer: I think the boy in the picture is telling the story because he says "I can bend." so he is talking about himself.
2. The words *bend*, *turn*, and *stretch* describe ways the body can move.
3. The boy is bending his body over to the left side. He is stretching his right arm up high. He is stretching his right side over to the left.
4. Students should circle: A. TRUE. The text tells us the boy likes to move.

We Need Water, pp. 8–9
1. The main idea of this text is that we need water for many things.
2. Students should say that *thirsty* means: A. dry.
3. Answers will vary. Sample answers: I used water to wash my hands and face. I used water to flush the toilet. I drank water. I used water to brush my teeth.
4. Students should say you can guess: A. You can use water to wash a dish.
5. Answers: A. drink, dry; B. bath, clean

I Protect Myself from Cold, pp. 10–11
1. The main idea is that people should protect themselves from the cold in the winter.
2. Yes, they are wearing hats, mitts, scarves, boots, and warm coats.
3. First, the author put on a warm coat and hat.
4. The word "finally" means "last."
5. If you get too cold, you should go inside.

Cover Sneezes and Coughs, pp. 12–13
1. The title tells me I will be reading about covering sneezing and coughing.
2. When you sneeze or cough, you spread germs.
3. The pictures help me to know what happens when you sneeze. They show what happens when you do not use a tissue, and when you do use a tissue.
4. Students should list two of the following: You can use a tissue when you sneeze. You can cover your mouth when you cough. You can cough or sneeze into your sleeve if you do not have a tissue.
5. The author is trying to teach the reader how to not spread germs when they are sick.
6. Answers may vary. Sample answers: Some students might say "Bless you." Others might say "Gesundheit."

No Peanuts for Me! pp. 14–15
1. The title of the text means that certain people cannot eat peanuts.
2. Students should list any three of the following: their skin gets red, their mouth tingles, their throat swells, they have problems breathing.
3. When someone needs help, you can tell an adult right away.
4. The picture shows a peanut in a circle with a line through it. That means no peanuts.
5. Answers may vary. Students may say they can bring only peanut-free foods to school.
6. The word *tingle* means: A. A stinging feeling.

Apples Are Good to Eat, pp. 16–17
1. The title of the text is Apples Are Good to Eat.
2. Students should list one of the following facts from the text: apples are good for you; some apples are red; some apples are green; some apples are yellow.
3. The author says it is fun to bite into an apple.
4. Students should choose: B. FALSE. Not all apples are red.
5. Answers will vary. Ensure that students give reasons why they do or do not like apples.
6. Answers will vary. Sample answers: apple sauce, apple juice, caramel apples, candy apples, apple crisp, apple cobbler, peanut butter sandwich with apple slices, apple slices with caramel dip, baked apples, apple muffins, in Waldorf salad, in fruit salad

Safe in the Sun, pp. 18–19
1. The text is about how to stay safe in the sun.
2. We protect skin from UV rays because they can burn skin.
3. Four ways to play safely in the sunshine are to wear sunscreen, wear a hat, wear sunglasses, and stay out of the sunshine (or play in the shade).
4. Sunscreen should be put on every 2 hours.
5. Answers might vary. Most students should say the girl looks as though she is at a beach.
6. Answers will vary. Students might say that the text reminds them of an ad for sunscreen or a medical poster warning about the dangers of too much sunshine.

Play Safely, pp. 20–21

1. We need rules to help us play safe and to have fun.
2. Students should list any two of the following rules for playing safe outside: wait your turn, sit down on swings and slides, tie up your shoes, wear sunscreen, be careful when it is wet.
3. A. Pam can get hurt.
4. Ensure that students' drawings show people sitting down on a swing, and other aspects of playing safe on a swing.

What Is a Smoke Detector? pp. 22–23

1. A smoke detector tells you when there is smoke from something burning.
2. The smoke detector beeps very loudly.
3. The checklist gives you short easy steps to remember to do when a smoke detector is beeping loudly.
4. Answers: First, go outside.
   Next, find an adult.
   Finally, ask for help.
5. Answers:
   B. FALSE
   A. TRUE

Who Keeps Me Safe? pp. 24–25

1. Police help me when I am lost. And they stop bad people.
2. Firefighters put out fires that could hurt me.
3. Doctors and nurses help when I am sick. They take care of me.
4. The pictures show who the text is talking about.
5. Ensure that students' pictures show a time when someone kept them safe.

Inky Dinky Spider, pp. 26–27

1. The song is about a little spider trying to climb up a water spout.
2. First, the spider climbs the water spout.
   Next, it rains and the spider gets washed out of the water spout.
   Then, the sun comes out and dries up the rain.
   Finally, the spider climbs back up the water spout again.
3. The sun dried up all the rain.
4. Answers might vary. Sample answers: Yes, I like the song because it is fun to sing and it has a happy ending. I also like doing the actions; No, I do not like the song because I do not like spiders.
5. Students should choose: B. FALSE.

One, Two, Buckle My Shoe, pp. 28–29

1. The name of the chant is One, Two, Buckle My Shoe.
2. To do up a buckle on a shoe.
3. The highest number in the chant is ten or 10.
4. For three and four, you shut the door.

5. Answers will vary. Students should list any two of the following: four and door; six and sticks; eight and straight; ten and hen.
6. The words for each blank in order are *buckle, shut, sticks, straight, fat hen.*

Where Does Trash Go? pp. 30–31

1. A landfill is a place where they take trash.
2. Students should list any of the following facts about landfills. Most trash goes to a landfill. Machines dig dirt to cover the trash in a landfill. People can help landfills by making less trash. Landfills can get filled up.
3. The first picture shows a man and truck picking up the trash. The second picture shows a machine moving the trash around in a landfill.
4. Students should check off all three boxes. To make less trash, you can use both sides of the paper, give clothes that do not fit you to smaller kids, and save leftover food for snacks.
5. Ensure that students' drawings show ways to make less trash. They might show recycling, reusing, or reducing.

Farmers, pp. 32–33

1. Farmers grow fruits and vegetables.
2. Meat comes from cows and chickens.
3. Truck drivers take the food to the stores.
4. Store clerks sell us the food.
5. Ensure that students' drawings show their family participating in cooking food together. Ensure that students write a sentence about their picture.

At the Park, pp. 34–35

1. The title tells me the text is about something that happens at the park.
2. The park is near the author's home.
3. The author plays on the slide first.
4. Answers will vary. Ensure that students give a reason why they like or do not like going to the park.
5. Answers might vary. Sample answer: I think the author likes going to the park because they have a lot of fun at the park.
6. Answers:
   A. slide
   B. swing

Out on the Lake, pp. 36–37

1. The title of the text is "Out on the Lake."
2. The author sees fish in the water.
3. An opinion from the story is: Being out on the lake on a summer day is fun!
4. Answers will vary. Sample answers: swim, play in the sand, look for shells, go fishing, jump the waves, build sand castles, run on the beach

5. The author says that some days there are lots of boats, and some days there is just our boat.

The Sun, pp. 38–39
1. The text is about how the Sun gives us light and heat.
2. The sentence that is a fact is: A. Every morning the Sun rises.
3. The opinion is: B. I love the warm sunshine on my skin!
4. Students should circle: A. TRUE. The Sun gives us heat.
5. The first thing that happens in the text is: A. The Sun rises.

Space, pp. 40–41
1. The title of the text is "Space."
2. The sentence that is a fact from the text is: B. I can see stars in space.
3. Students should circle: A. TRUE. Planets are in space.
4. The words "shooting star" mean: A. A star that moves quickly across the sky.
5. In space the author can see the Moon, stars, and shooting stars.

About Seeds, pp. 42–43
1. The text tells me a seed is a tiny plant waiting to grow.
2. Seeds need sun, water, and soil to grow.
3. The two special parts talked about in the text are fluff on dandelion seeds and wings on maple tree seeds.
4. Students should list two of the following types of seeds from the text: a peanut, a coconut, a dandelion seed with fluff on it, and a maple tree seed with wings on it.
5. The fact that we learned from the text is: A. Seeds need sun, water, and soil to grow.

What Is a Cactus? pp. 44–45
1. Answers will vary. Sample answers: I learned that cactus needles are called spines. I learned that some cactuses are taller than a house and some are smaller than golf balls.
2. A cactus is a plant.
3. Most cactuses live in the desert.
4. *Spines* are sharp needles that grow on cactuses.
5. The word *desert* means: B. A place where it does not rain much.
6. You may wish to make a bulletin board display of students' drawings.

Sara's Flower Garden, pp. 46–47
1. The two things Sara does with the seeds are she plants them in the soil with care, and she waters the seeds to help them grow.

2. The sentence that is a fact from the story is A. Sara has a flower garden.
3. Sample answer: Yes, I think Sara likes her garden. I know because she is happy when the flowers grow and she likes the red flowers.
4. After Sara waters the seeds, they grow into tall plants.
5. Students should circle: B. FALSE. Sara likes the red flowers best.

How People Use Plants, pp. 48–49
1. The main idea of this text is that people use plants in many ways.
2. Students should choose: A. TRUE. Trees are plants.
3. Answers will vary. Sample answers: My favourite things to eat that come from plants are tomatoes, strawberries, maple syrup, potatoes, kiwis, and oranges.
4. Students should list any two of the following facts about plants from the text: People use plants. Plants give us food. Trees are plants. Wood comes from trees.
5. Students should list any two of the following ways that people use wood: People build houses with wood. People burn wood for heat. People make hockey sticks and baseball bats from wood.

Why Plant a Tree? pp. 50–51
1. Trees clean the air we breathe.
2. Trees protect us from the sun and wind.
3. Trees give animals a place to live and food to eat.
4. Answers will vary. Sample answer: The tree foods I eat are peaches, plums, apples, walnuts, and maple syrup.
5. The picture shows a girl planting a young tree.
6. Students should list 4 of the following ways trees help: trees clean the air we breath, protect us from sun and wind, give animals a place to live and food to eat, some trees give us food such as fruits and nuts.

How to Be a Good Friend, pp. 52–53
1. The author is trying to teach the reader what you should do to be a good friend.
2. Students should list any four of the following ways to be a good friend: be kind, listen to what they say, stick up for them, share your toys and games with them, take turns when playing games with them, and playing fair with them.
3. The picture shows being kind.
4. Sample answer: I might say "I like your hat." or "Nice hat!" Ensure that students' pictures show them being a good friend.
5. Answers will vary.

Ways to Be Kind, pp. 54–55

1. Answers will vary. Sample answers: How to Be Kind, Being Kind to Others, Being Kind
2. The picture shows a boy at school holding the door open for a teacher. She is carrying a large box.
3. Ensure that students write five ways to be kind.
4. Students should put a check mark beside "Take care of a friend's toys," and "Follow the rules at school."

Play Fair, pp. 56–57

1. The main idea is that everyone should play fair and not get mad when playing games with friends.
2. Students should choose: B. FALSE. The text says it is fun to play with Val.
3. Someone is a good sport when they do not get mad when playing a game with others. The second cartoon shows Val being a good sport.
4. Val played fair when she stopped herself from getting mad when Jon tagged her.
5. Ensure that students draw some aspect of playing fair.

Julie Payette, pp. 58–59

1. Students should choose: B. Watching space missions on TV.
2. The plane Julie flew in was special because being on the plane was like being in space.
3. Students should choose: A. Someone who travels in space.
4. Students should choose: A. Go on the International Space Station.
5. Julie learned to fly two types of planes as part of her training to go into space.

Chris Hadfield, pp. 60–61

1. Chris is an astronaut. He travels in space.
2. The caption says that Chris played his guitar in space.
3. Answers will vary.
4. Students should choose: B. FALSE. Chris did not travel in space when he was a boy.
5. Students should circle: B. Chris took many pictures in space.

Alexander Graham Bell, pp. 62–63

1. This story is about an inventor named Alexander Graham Bell.
2. The word *invent* means to make something new.
3. The fact from the text is: A. Alexander invented the telephone.
4. Alexander liked to invent things and build machines. He also liked helping people.
5. You can tell Alexander was a nice man because he liked to help people.

My Trip to a Farm, pp. 64–65

1. Kyle wrote the email.
2. Kyle's grandma will get the email.
3. Kyle is telling the story. Kyle tells what he did at the farm.
4. Kyle went to a farm.
5. Students should draw a pie.

What Animals Eat, pp. 66–67

1. Animals need to eat food so they can grow.
2. Students should choose any two of the following foods: plants, soft branches, buds, leaves, seeds, and meat.
3. The word *munch* means: B. To eat.
4. Students should choose: B. FALSE. Bears do not eat twigs.
5. Students' drawings should show an animal eating food.

Taking Care of a Pet, pp. 68–69

1. The main idea of the text is the ways to take care of a pet.
2. Answers will vary. Ensure that students list 3 of the following points: feed it every day, make sure it has water, give it exercise, play with it, be kind to it, take it to the veterinarian when it is sick.
3. A veterinarian can help an animal that is sick. A veterinarian examines the animal and gives it medicine to help it get better.
4. Answers will vary. Sample answers: I would like to help cats because I like to see them happy and purring. I would like to help dogs because I like to see them wag their tails.

My Cat Boots, pp. 70–71

1. This text is about a pet cat named Boots and what she likes to do.
2. Answers will vary. Students should list any two of the following: Boots likes to play, she likes to chase little balls, she likes to be fed.
3. When Boots wants to be fed, she meows, and jumps in the person's lap.
4. Students should draw Boots chasing little balls or eating.

My Dog Jake, pp. 72–73

1. Special things Jake can do are he can do tricks, he can shake hands, and he can play catch.
2. The sentence found in the text is: B. Jake can do many tricks.
3. The author says about Jake that: B. He is the best pet ever!
4. Answers will vary. Sample answers: Yes, I would like a pet dog. I love to play with dogs! No, I would not like a pet dog. I am allergic to dogs.

5. Ensure that students' drawings show their dog or a pet they would like to have.

Ducks and Geese, pp. 74–75

1. Sample answer: Ducks and geese are birds. The text tells me they have wings and feathers, and I know birds have wings and feathers.
2. Students should choose one of the following facts about ducks: Ducks can be many different colours. Ducks like to swim in the water. Ducks are smaller than geese. Ducks have wings and feathers.
3. Students should choose one of the following facts about geese: Geese are mostly white, grey, black, or brown. Geese also swim in the water. Geese have wings and feathers. Students may also infer that geese are larger than ducks.
4. Students should choose one of the following ways ducks and geese are alike: Ducks and geese are alike because they both have wings and feathers, and they both like to swim in the water.
5. Students should choose one of the following ways ducks and geese are different: ducks are smaller than geese. Ducks can be many different colours, but geese are mostly white, grey, black or brown.
6. Answers: A. wings, feathers

Fish Facts, pp. 76–77

1. Fish live in the water. They live in lakes, ponds, rivers, and oceans.
2. Fish move by flapping their fins and tail.
3. Answers will vary. Ensure that students give reasons why they would or would not like a fish for a pet.
4. Students should choose: A. TRUE. Tuna are fish.
5. Ensure that students' drawings are of a fish. Ensure that students include a sentence describing their fish.

Mighty Moles, pp. 78–79

1. The title tells you that moles are strong.
2. A mole's furry coat would help it stay warm.
3. Students should choose: B. FALSE. Moles are not large animals.
4. From the text, you can guess that: A. Worms live in the ground.
5. The sentence that is a fact from the text is: A. Moles have sharp claws.

You Can Write an Email, pp. 80–81

1. The text is about writing an email and the parts of an email.
2. From top to bottom, the spaces should be labelled as *addresses, subject, message, your name.*
3. Answers will vary, but most students should know someone who writes emails.

You Can Write a Postcard, pp. 82–83

1. The postcard shows a picture of the Peace Tower in Ottawa.
2. Ensure that students' drawings show a place they have visited.
3. Ensure that students' postcards tell about the place in their drawings.

This Is January, pp. 84–85

1. Yes, the picture shows the month of January on a calendar.
2. The month of January starts the year. January has 31 days.
3. Pam's birthday is on January 17.
4. Answers will vary.
5. Ensure that students label the correct month and day for their individual birthday.

Summer Days, pp. 86–87

1. A fact from the text is: A. Summer days are sunny and hot.
2. Sample answer: Yes, I think the author likes summer. I know because the author says "I love summer!"
3. The author looks for shells on the beach.
4. The author sees fish in the water.
5. Encourage students to add interesting details to their beach scene, such as sand castles, and colourful beach toys, umbrellas, and towels.

One Fall Day, pp. 88–89

1. The text is about what it is like in the fall.
2. The person in the story wears a sweater outside in the fall.
3. The fall leaves are red and yellow.
4. Students might say they have seen leaves that were orange, brown, and green in the fall.
5. The author helps their mom rake the leaves.
6. Answers will vary. Ensure that students include an explanation.

How Toy Ads Work, pp. 90–91

1. The ad is selling a set of emergency vehicles called Hero Wheels—an ambulance, a police car, a helicopter, and a fire truck.
2. It gets your attention with the big letters, the star with the words in it, and the ribbon or award.
3. The ad says "Be #1 with Hero Wheels," "New This Year!" and "Be a Hero!" The ad tells you the names of the vehicles. The ad also tells you there are four models to choose from.
4. The author gives information. They are telling all about the four toys you can buy. They are not telling you a story about them.

5. Yes: the ad says there are four models and it shows four vehicles; the ad says they are new so they probably are
No: just because you have this toy does not mean you are a hero or #1
6. A. words, pictures
B. look, ad.

I Have Money, pp. 92–93

1. The main idea of the text is to show the different coins and tell how much they are worth.
2. The pictures show the different coins and tell what each coin is worth.
3. The text uses words to tell how much each coin is worth. The pictures use numbers and symbols to tell how much each coin is worth.
4. There are five coins.
5. The nickel is worth 5¢, the dime is worth 10¢, the quarter is worth 25¢, the loonie is worth $1 or 100¢, and the toonie is worth $2 or 200¢. The total amount is 5 + 10 + 25 + 100 + 200 = 340¢ or $3.40.
6. Answers may vary. Students can show any of the following: 6 nickels, 4 nickels and 1 dime, 2 nickels and 2 dimes, 3 dimes, 1 quarter and 1 nickel.

Mixing Colours, pp. 94–95

1. The author is trying to teach the reader about mixing certain colours to make other colours.
2. The four colours you need to mix paints are red, white, yellow, and blue.
3. When you mix yellow and blue, you get green.
4. Ensure that students' drawings show the red and blue colours separately, then mixing into purple.
5. Red + white = pink

Clouds, pp. 96–97

1. The main idea of the text is that the author likes to watch what clouds look like and what they do.
2. Answers will vary. Ensure that students give reasons why they do or do not like to watch clouds.
3. No, not all clouds bring rain. I know because the text says that grey clouds bring rain and snow. Clouds can also be white, so that means white clouds do not bring rain.
4. Answers:
B. FALSE. No clouds are green.
A. TRUE. Some clouds bring rain or snow.
A. TRUE. Clouds float in the sky.
5. You can see clouds that are pink and blue when the sun is setting in the evening.

Make Some Noise! pp. 98–99

1. The sentence that is a fact from the text is: B. On New Year's Eve, people yell "Happy New Year!"
2. Answers will vary. Sample answers: Yes, fireworks are fun to watch because they are beautiful colours and patterns. They also make loud booms and cracking sounds. No, I do not think fireworks are fun to watch. They are very loud and noisy, and they scare me.
3. Answers will vary.
4. Sample answers: On New Year's Eve, people yell, blow horns, eat, sing, have fun, play games, and more.
5. Ensure that students draw a picture of fireworks. Encourage students to use plenty of bright colours.

Using Text Features—Table of Contents, pp. 100–101

1. The title of the book is Farm Animals.
2. Farmer Brown is the author.
3. There are six chapters in the book.
4. The title of Chapter 5 is Horses.
5. The title of Chapter 2 is Chickens.
6. Chapter 6 tells about the barn.
7. Chapter 4 is about cows.
8. Chapter 3 is about pigs.